The Cry of the Prophet

A CALL TO FULLNESS OF LIFE

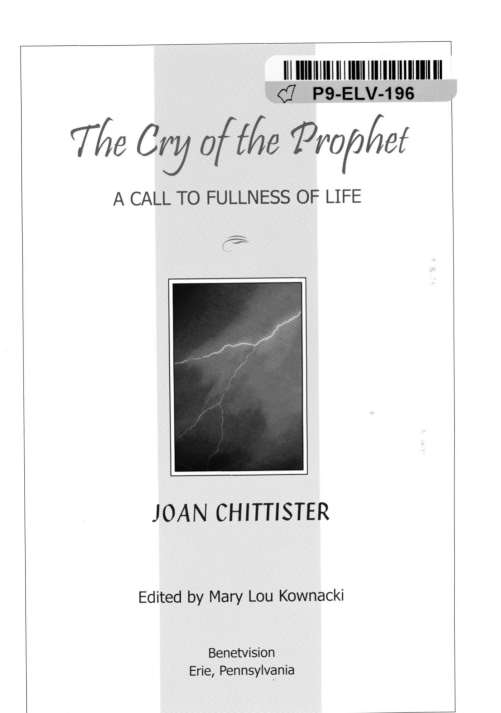

JOAN CHITTISTER

Edited by Mary Lou Kownacki

Benetvision
Erie, Pennsylvania

$7.00
Quantity discounts available.

Benetvision
355 East Ninth Street
Erie, PA 16503-1107

Phone: 814-459-5994   Fax: 814-459-8066
benetvision@benetvision.org
www.benetvision.org

Benetvision exists to encourage the development of contemporary spirituality from a feminist, global and monastic perspective through the works of Joan Chittister.

ISBN: 978 1-890890-25-4

09 10 11 12 4 3 2 1

Table of Contents

INTRODUCTION

What Are Prophets?

What this world needs most right now is a new generation of prophets. The problem is that we have lost all respect for them. In fact, we may not even recognize them when we see them.

Yet, it was precisely for times such as ours that God sent the prophets. It is surely time for this generation to rediscover them.

We aren't, after all, the only people who have gone through such social disorientation, such moral confusion. We aren't the only people in history who have put down our ideals in favor of our desires. We aren't the only people in the world who have wanted more comfort than challenge, more money than community, more power than equality.

The word "prophet" rings with a hard edge these days, a memory of denunciation that comes with a shudder and the urge to take a step backwards. We shrink from the very idea of the prophetic dimension of religion or, at best, relegate the idea of it to times past when God bent stiff necks with mighty swords. We shrink from the very thought of raising our voices above the crowd. We want a religion that chants but never howls, that prays but never brings the foolish standards of the Gospel to the issues of the time.

What a shame. All we prove in our sterile dash to be "polite" and "civil" and "reasonable" about faith is how little we know of prophets and prophecy these days. How little we understand the role of gospel critique in a world where people expect to talk religion but not to do it, who will define religion but do not want to steer by it, who will argue religion but do not want to apply it to the here and now, to the this and that, to modern life as well as to ancient myth. Prophecy we assume for times of mystical allegory but not for moments of major upheaval in our own worlds, great and small, public and personal.

We like to separate the prophets of the church from the people of the church. We like to separate ourselves from the demands of greatness. But the prophetic dimensions of the church, Scripture demonstrates in its greatest prophetic figures of Amos, Hosea, Isaiah, Micah, and Ezekiel, are simple souls just like us: ordinary citizens, compassionate lovers, justice-seeking and persistent idealists who move with courage into places that everyone else takes for granted, and speak God's word in the midst of human chaos loudly, clearly, courageously, whatever the levy it imposes on their own lives. Prophecy, in other words, is not a luxury; it is an essential dimension of the Christian life. We will not be forgiven our disdain of holy risk in the name of weakness.

Nazim Hikmet, in the environment spawned by World War II, wrote: "This life is not a joke. You must take it seriously. Seriously enough to find yourself up against a wall, perhaps, with your hands bound." The statement is a call to prophets without portfolio. The question is, however, what can possibly be worth doing with so much passion? What can possibly need to be done in our world with such commitment? And how do we know that what we are doing has that kind of eternal meaning?

The answers, I think, lie in looking again at what prophets came to prophesy and why, and asking whether or not their messages have been heard.

Amos
The Prophet in the Mirror

Scripture

The words of Amos, a sheep breeder from Tekoa.
These are the visions Amos had of Israel in the time
of Uzziah ruler of Judah and of Jeroboam ben-Joash,
ruler of Israel, two years before the earthquake.

Amos 1:1

I despise and reject your feasts!
    I am not appeased by your solemn assemblies!
When you offer me burnt offerings,
    I reject your oblations,
    and refuse to look at your sacrifices
    of fattened cattle!
Spare me the racket of your chanting!
    Relieve me of the strumming of your harps!
Rather, let justice flow like a river,
    and righteousness flow like an unfailing stream.

Amos 5: 21-24

Response

Find a work of art or a picture or a story in this week's media—newspaper, internet, TV—that speaks to you about this week's Scripture. Explain.

READING

The Prophet Amos

by Joan Chittister

The prophet is not a mental derangement gone amuck in the streets. In fact, the wild-eyed and unbalanced need not apply. Some of the finest, most stable and least extroverted people in salvation history have been called to prophecy and witness. Moses, for instance, had great misgivings about finding himself stripped psychologically naked and alone in the political snake pit of the times. Mary of Nazareth had no preparation whatsoever for the task of confronting an entire system with the presence of Jesus. Martin Luther King, Jr., a newly ordained young minister, felt very ill prepared to defy a racist nation. No doubt about it, if prophecy takes anything at all, it takes great emotional balance, rugged mental health. If anything, the people God sends to call us to our spiritual senses erase from sight completely whatever image of the mangy and berserk we have carried in our souls and called "prophet."

Most of the prophets, what's more, are certainly not mystics; many of them are not even unusually pious people. They claim a "word" but seldom a vision. None of them have been religious fanatics. On the contrary, all of them have been rather average types who kept their hand to the plow and their souls on course. They were hardworking and spiritually steady, seekers of the first degree. Nowhere does the Scripture say that they themselves were privately or personally perfect, at least not according to the religious standards around them, but one thing is certain: they knew clearly what God wanted for their world and they never forgot what God expected of them.

A Prophet Is Normal

The prophet Amos was Mr. Normalcy. He was the man down the street in the modest little house with the awnings, the garden and the wrought iron fence. Self-employed. Financially secure. Politically independent. And very, very aware of what was going on around him. He was a simple man with powerful, God-given insight. He owned his own vineyards; he tended his own sheep. He was just like everybody else, except that he wasn't. Amos thought very differently from others. And he said so. That was his first mistake. He was just like the people around him. What right did he have to tell anybody anything. The fact is that Amos prophesied to a world that was totally satisfied with itself.

In the time of Amos, Israel flourished. The country gorged itself on the goods of the world. Israel stood at its most powerful and prosperous peak since the time of King David, Israel's greatest, most charismatic leader. Life was good. The boundaries of the nation extended farther than they ever had before. Production and profits were up. As far as the merchants and the military and the monarch were concerned, Yahweh was blessing Israel.

Amos, in other words, found himself completely akin but totally out of step with his times. Amos saw the wealth, of course, but he had the effrontery to question where the power and prosperity of Israel had come from and what the Israelites had done to gain it. In answer, Amos cited war crimes and tax foreclosures and "failures at the gate," where the elders of the city assembled to mete out justice but where, too often, they decided against the poor in favor of the rich and powerful.

The Same but Different

It was a curiously debauched society that Amos saw around him—and a falsely pious one. While the poor were being overlooked, overcharged, overwhelmed by the corruption and dishonesty around them, worship continued at great pace and in grandiose style at the great shrines. "Do not seek out Bethel; do not go to Gilgal; do not journey to Beer-Sheba," Amos warned the pilgrims and the pious. "Let justice reign at the city gate."

But no one listened.

Their theology told them that they were special to God. Their worship told them that they were faithful to God. Its regularity alone, if nothing else, lulled them into thinking that their relationship with God was intact. And, in a society that believed that God punished sinners and blessed saints in kind—their wealth itself, stolen from the poor and hoarded by the rich, they took as sign that God was pleased with them. It was a pleasantly warped approach to the fundamentals of morality that made the wages of sin the sign of virtue. And Amos saw it and denounced it. Israel, he said with damning insight, was no better than any other nation around them. Amos was normal, yes, but Amos was different as well. Amos cared enough about what was going on to question it.

A Cry for Justice

And now and here what would an Amos see?

Amos would see that here, too, justice weeps; the basics of human decency are bartered; the human covenant slacks and sags and breaks.

In a world where excessive violence is our stock in trade, our pride, our economic base as chief military merchant to the world, the blood of our own children runs in our own streets because we have taught them violence well.

In a society where, from the largest US cities to the smallest towns the numbers of hungry and homeless increase daily while churchgoing continues to rise, the message of the prophet Amos, spoken from the countryside to the heart of the temple, goes yet unheard. Here, too, among us, Amos, "the shepherd and dresser of sycamore trees"—the farmer, the average seeker with a holy heart—is indeed a poet in demand.

Nothing has changed. Ritual is still not the essence of religion. The society that does not do justice to its widows, its poor and its children lives a lie however well it lives, however moral it appears.

No, nothing has changed perhaps, but something must. This time your voice and mine, the voice of average, normal caring people, must again sound the prophetic knell or the memory of the mind of God may well be lost to the land forever.

A Call to Prophesy

It's a hard lesson, this awareness that what we know in our hearts to be the will of God we must speak in the light. It is a lesson we try consistently to avoid. We don't rock boats. We don't talk politics. We don't mind other people's business. We go along.

We are not the prophetic type. Neither are the people in the neighborhood. Nor are the people in the parish. Nor are the people in our family. Nor are we. And yet, it is to our normal little worlds that each of us is called to be prophet now as Amos was then.

Indeed, just when we convince ourselves that disturbing dinner parties is not what we're about, there in front of us stands Amos. He was a private person, not a professional religious. He was uneducated in a sophisticated world. He was well-to-do in a society of have-nots. He was a global visionary in a nationalistic world. And with those gifts he did what he could to make the world a better place. He demanded justice from the judges. He preached in the temple what the priest, to curry favor, would not say about the policies of the king. He spared nothing and no one from the heat of God's light. He knew what it meant to be told that such things were not his business, yet, driven by the Word of God, he made them the stuff of the spiritual life.

As long as the work of God on earth is yet undone, Amos's prophetic cry is to the prophet in each of us, muted for years now, perhaps, but forever on call. Who knows? It may be precisely you and your insights, your very average voice and your clear-hearted vision for which the world now waits.

Discussion

1. Think of three people you know. Do you ever see "a prophet" in them? Explain.

2. Name one time that you spoke up in a public gathering for the poor, for disarmament, women in the church, for any unpopular cause. What did it cost you?

3. Write a prophecy similar to Amos 5: 21-24 (see this week's Scripture) comparing the religious rituals and pieties of our time to what is happening to the poor in our neighborhoods, cities, country and world.

ECHOES: WOMEN PROPHETS

When I am hungry and I eat a good meal for the glory of God, it is a work of mercy.... It is all the more a work of mercy when I grow, reap, peel, cook, or serve a square meal for my family or wash the dishes afterwards, or sweep the kitchen, or take out the garbage. It is all the more a work of mercy when I do it for strangers, and still more so when I do it for my enemies.

Ade Bethune

When everyone was terrorized we didn't stay at home crying—we went to the streets to confront them directly. We were mad, but it was the only way to stay sane.

Mothers of the Disappeared who confronted the brutal military rule in Argentina (1976-83) with a weekly, silent public vigil on behalf of family members who "were disappeared."

I know what I want, I have a goal, an opinion, I have a religion and love. Let me be myself and then I am satisfied. I
know that I'm a woman, a woman with inward strength and
plenty of courage. If God lets me live...I shall not remain in-
significant, I shall work in the world and for mankind! And
now I know that first and foremost I shall require courage
and cheerfulness.

Anne Frank

When I first found out I had cancer, I didn't know what to
pray for. I didn't know if I should pray for healing or life or
death. Then I found peace in praying for what my folks call
"God's perfect will." As it evolved, my prayer has become,
"Lord, let me live until I die." By that I mean I want to live,
love, and serve fully until death comes. If that prayer is
answered...how long really doesn't matter. Whether it's just
a few months or a few years is really immaterial.

Thea Bowman

Response

Which of the voices of women prophets spoke to you most clearly? Explain.

PHOTO and POEM MEDITATION

Sit with this photo a few minutes and read the poem.

Call and Answer

by Robert Bly

Tell me why it is we don't lift our voices these days
And cry over what is happening. Have you noticed
The plans are made for Iraq and the ice cap is melting?

I say to myself: "Go on, cry. What's the sense
of being an adult and having no voice? Cry out!
See who will answer! This is Call and Answer!"

We will have to call especially loud to reach
Our angels, who are hard of hearing; they are hiding
In the jugs of silence filled during our wars.

Have we agreed to so many wars that we can't
Escape from silence? If we don't lift our voices, we allow
Others (who are ourselves) to rob the house.

How come we've listened to the great criers—Neruda,
Akhmatova, Thoreau, Frederick Douglass—and now
We're silent as sparrows in the little bushes?

Some masters say our life lasts only seven days.
Where are we in the week? Is it Thursday yet?
Hurry, cry now! Soon Sunday night will come.

Creative Response

Individual:
Spend 5 to 10 minutes looking into a mirror. Have a conversation with the prophet that lives in you.

Group:
1. Place a mirror in front of each person in the group. Read the poem "Call and Answer" aloud. Ask each person to look into the mirror and finish the phrase "I am crying out for...." Have the participants voice their cries aloud.

2. Break into groups of three or four and dramatize the poem by Robert Bly.

WEEK TWO

Hosea
Love without Limit

Scripture

When YHWY first spoke to Hosea, YHYW said: "Go! Marry a prostitute and beget children of prostitution! For the land is guilty of the most hideous kind of prostitution by forsaking YHWH." So Hosea married Gomer bat-Diblaim, who conceived and bore a son.

Hosea 1: 2,3

After that, however, I will woo her;
    I will lead her into the desert,
    speaking tenderly to her heart.
On that day I will make a covenant for them
    with the beasts of the field and with the birds of the air,
    and with the creeping things that move about the earth.
I will smash the bow and sword
    and abolish war from the land,
    so that all may sleep in safety.
 I will bind myself to you in love forever—
    yes, I will swear myself to you in rightness and justice,
    in tender love and in deep compassion.
I will swear myself to you in love and faithfulness,
    and then you will truly know YHWH.

Hosea 2: 16, 20-21

Response

Find a work of art or a picture or a story in this week's media—newspaper, internet, TV—that speaks to you about this week's Scripture. Explain.

READING

The Prophet Hosea

by Joan Chittister

When we think of prophets we conjure up images of howling hurts and eyes of steel. What we fail to see in the prophet's eyes and hear in the prophet's howl is the rage that comes when, seeing pain, a person stands helpless in its wake. The prophet's wail is the cry of despair that comes from those who stand in front of a burning building powerless to put out the flame. The prophet's shriek rises out of the angst of helplessness that stops the breath of the living at the bedside of the dead. The prophet does not cry against us; the prophet cries for us.

Judgment, you see, comes from compassion. Compassion, in fact, demands judgment so that the sufferer may be liberated and the suffering may be scourged. The prophet in society carries the burden of both judgment and compassion. To have one without the other is not to prophesy at all.

Avengers without love are not prophets. At the same time, lovers without a sense of accountability are not prophets either. The prophetic figure brings to a situation full of despair the face of feeling and the face of hope, the one who suffers because of us and believes in us at the same time. The prophet drags us by the hair of the head, if necessary, to the heights of our capacity and against our own worst will. The prophet comes with a father's zeal and a mother's love breathing the word of God and saying "I love you" at the same time.

The model of compassion and judgment that God gives to those who find themselves faced with something they hate in something they love is the prophet Hosea, a sad and sorry prototype of a God who has also been betrayed. Hosea, like God, has been betrayed by someone he loved beyond all the boundaries of good sense and right reason. And it hurts. Hosea, like God, is a loving fool, a foolish lover whose hurt never diminishes his love and whose love never discounts the hurt and its need to be cauterized.

Hosea's story is the story of anyone who loves a country or a church or a way of life or a family recklessly, without limits, yet without denying the hard truth about it that cuts to the quick. Some good things grieve us, fail to live up to what they have promised to be, go soft in the middle, flirt with the edges of their integrity. Then, judgment is called for; and in the judgment, compassion is required or, instead of healing, there is only surgery for its own sake. Hosea is a model of justice tempered by compassion.

Message Unheard

Hosea lived in a period and a place where the priests of the temple had become tamed and fattened on the spoils of the system. The temple had gone political, profiting from the system but never, ever calling it to account. It was the word of the king, not the Word of Yahweh that mattered. It was sacrifice and cult and culture that mattered to the priests, not insight and wisdom and the justice of *tsedakah* (righteousness). It was the practice of religion, not the righteousness of religion that counted now.

"My people perish for want of knowledge," Hosea lamented, when the teachers of truth, the priests of the temple, played at being ministers by sacrificing animals, by maintaining rituals, but questioned nothing about the truth of the teachings of the time. The priests went along with the practices of the religion but never required the religion itself to be religious.

And who doesn't know that it is no small thing to see a church go political, to discover that pastors prefer full collections to full homilies, to find out that ministers preach the civil religion more than they do the Christian religion, to discover that the church that teaches the value of creation discounts half of it as less worthy than the other half.

It is no small moment for the soul to come face-to-face with the fact that it is a politicized religion that puts the flag of the country in the sanctuary and holy places. It is a politicized religion that buys its tax exempt status with silence and holds prayer breakfasts instead of protests while civil rights legislation erodes away and minorities are left to wonder about a God who prefers the body politic to the mystical body. It is a totally politicized church that cedes the teaching of the just war theory to the commander in chief of the armed forces.

Clearly, Hosea's message to a domesticated church is a potent but a missing one, even in our own lifetimes.

Loving Criticism

But, as important as it is, that is not Hosea's only message to us. The real message of Hosea's prophetic life is that Hosea loves honestly and Hosea loves foolishly. Hosea knows that Gomer, his wife, has been unfaithful to him but Hosea loves her regardless. And therein lies the prophet's call: not simply to condemn what once you loved but to love what must be condemned and to condemn it lovingly.

There is a major difference between a critic and a prophet. Critics stand outside a system and mock it. Prophets remain clear-eyed and conscientious inside a sinful system and love it anyway. It is easy to condemn the country, for instance. It is possible to criticize the church. But it is prophetic to love both church and country enough to want them to be everything they claim to be—just, honest, free, equal—and then to stay with them in their faltering attempts to do so even if it is you yourself against whom both church and state turn in their attempts to evade the prophetic truth of the time.

The French papacy at Avignon did not want to hear the call of Catherine of Sienna but, in the end, she prevailed and they returned the Holy See to Rome. The powers that be did not want to hear Joan of Arc and killed her to silence her, but in the end, her prophetic word outlasted them all. Neither church nor state wanted to hear Dorothy Day and Thomas Merton in their pleas for the poor and their prophetic cry for peace, but in the end, it is their messages that expose the secularization of the church, that haunt it at the turn of every gospel page, that challenge it to this day and that have marked its best presence in these times.

The lesson of Hosea, then, is an important one for us, too. Criticize we must, but we cannot criticize what we do not love. Criticism without love is reproof for its own sake, power wielded brutishly, punishment with no power to save. The function of the prophet is not to destroy. The function of the prophet is to expose whatever cancers fester beneath the surface so what is loved can be saved while there is yet time.

To claim then that to criticize the government is treason, to insist that to criticize the church is disunity may be the greatest perfidy and the deepest infidelity of all. It is a prophet's lot to risk both so that what is worth loving can be lovable again.

"A coward is incapable of exhibiting love," Gandhi wrote. "It is the prerogative of the brave." It is the prerogative of those who are willing to pay the price of being a prophet. The horrible truth is that prophecy is not a harsh and heartless thing at all. Prophecy is unrequited love gone mad with hope.

Discussion

1. How do you understand the prophet's two-edged call to bring both compassion and judgment, love and condemnation to an unjust situation? Have you ever seen it in action? Explain.

2. Do you agree with Hosea and Chittister's reflection that the church has become "domesticated, tamed, fattened, politicized?" If so, write a letter to a church official about one issue that troubles you. For example, the practice of ritual rather than religion; too much church wealth; preference for the wealthy over the poor; timidity in calling the government to task about war and other social issues; sermons that put love of God and love of the flag on equal footing; inequality of women, etc. Try to do it with judgment and compassion. You can file the letter, tear it up, read it to a friend or send it.

3. Do you admire, pity, question, or disagree with Hosea's foolish love of Gomer, his "unrequited love gone mad with hope"? Can you think of a character in literature or a person in real life who loves or loved this way? Do you think God loves this way?

ECHOES: WOMEN PROPHETS

If you love the justice of Jesus Christ more than you fear human judgment then you will seek to do compassion. Compassion means that if I see my friend and my enemy in equal need, I shall help both equally. Justice demands that we seek and find the stranger, the broken, the prisoner, and comfort them and offer them our help. Here lies the holy compassion of God....

Mechthild of Magdeburg

Wherever Jesus went, he created abundance.

Jose Hobday

The only thing we can offer to God of value is to give our love to people as unworthy of it as we are of God's love.

St. Catherine of Sienna

You say you don't want anything to happen to me. I'd prefer it that way myself–but I don't see that we have control over the forces of madness, and if you choose to enter into other people's suffering, or love others, you at least have to consent in some way to the possible consequences.

Ita Ford
(Maryknoll Sister murdered in El Salvador)

Response

Which of the voices of women prophets spoke to you most clearly? Explain.

PHOTO and POEM MEDITATION

Sit with this photo a few minutes and read the poem.

The Way They Held Each Other

by Mira

A woman and her young daughter
were destitute
and traveling to another country
where they hoped to find
a new life.

Three men stole them while they were camping.

They were brought to a city
and sold as slaves; each to a different
owner.

They were given one minute more together,
before their fates became unknown.

My soul clings to God like that,
the way they held
each other.

Creative Response

Individual:
Interview 3 to 5 people—friends, family, parishioners, strangers—on the question: "What is a prophet?" Ask them to name a few prophets. Don't argue. Just listen, ask questions and record their answers.

Group:
1. Bring the data from your individual interviews to the group meeting. Discuss the answers of the people you interviewed in light of this reading. Decide on a group action after the discussion.

2. Break into groups of three or four. Dramatize Mira's poem or a section of it.

WEEK THREE

Isaiah
Steadfast in the Face of Adversity

Scripture

Then I heard the voice of the Holy One saying,
"Whom shall I send? Who will go for us?"
"Here I am," I said, "send me!"

Isaiah 6:8

But now, Leah and Rachel and Jacob,
    hear the word of YHWH –
the One who created you,
    the One who fashioned you, Israel:
Do not be afraid, for I have redeemed you;
    I have called you by name; you are mine.
When you pass through the seas, I will be with you;
    when you pass over the rivers, you will not drown.
Walk through fire, and you will not be singed;
    walk through flames and you will not be burned.
Have no fear, for I am with you.

Isaiah 43: 1-2, 5

Response

Find a work of art or a picture or story in this week's media—newspaper, internet, TV—that speaks about this week's Scripture. Explain.

The Prophet Isaiah

by Joan Chittister

Endurance shines as the hallmark of the prophets, the lode stone of the prophetic. Those who are willing to endure when endurance looks insane, has no hope of prevailing, consumes everything else in its path, are those who know a greater truth, a more promising hope, a truer way to wholeness than the world around them has to offer. That kind of endurance is of God. It transcends human concerns and demands human attention. That kind of endurance holds on to the divine in life even when life itself gives in to making gods of gold in deserts of sand. Prophetic endurance holds on, cries out, speaks up, stands pat whatever the pressure, however long the time, until, whether or not they agree, people listen and think.

Prophetic endurance is made out of stiffer steel than political approval and social acceptance. Prophetic endurance lasts far beyond its time, makes itself an irritating presence, holds the real up to the ideal until the sight of the contrast hurts.

The endurance of prophets demands the kind of dogged commitment that refuses to conform to anything less than the mind of God for the people of the world. This is a time for normal, compassionate people to foster endurance as well.

It is a dangerous moment in United States history. The real and the ideal are in constant conflict around us. What we tell ourselves we are about as a society, history far too often belies.

Is the situation salvageable? Can lost ideals be reclaimed in the face of a rampant and deteriorating realism? Of course they can. The names of hope are legion among us. But the moral decline of the society as a whole can only be finally and fully reversed on one condition: that we each learn to turn moral concern into prophetic endurance. Each of us must speak up, speak out and speak for justice and peace at every bridge club, every town meeting, every private party. We must persist until we become again what we have always wanted to be, until we all stand more for the truths of the gospel than for the goals of the government.

But where shall we go for such a model of sanctifying insight, social consciousness and holy endurance? Scripture leaves us no doubt. In addition to the normalcy of Amos and the compassion of Hosea, God raised up for our emulation the endurance of the prophet Isaiah.

Isaiah lived in a period of massive military power and political imperialism. For the first time in history, technological sophistication of enormous proportion had revolutionized the arena of national conflict. Equipment unheard of before Isaiah's time now enabled attacking armies to build ramps to the tops of city walls. Battering rams of awesome weight could now be beaten against the city gates. Archers armed with precision bows stood in disciplined ranks, ready to make a professional job of war. Whole cities could now be breached. Whole populations—the women and the children, the grandmothers and the old men, the sick and the blind, the peaceful and the unwary, the confused and the pliant—could now be slaughtered in the name of national honor.

And in the face of it all, Isaiah ran naked through the city for three years to save a people that, in the long run, fell prey to its own arrogance despite his efforts to command their attention. Israel "ate, drank and made merry," sure of its divine election and sunk up to its heart in divine reprobation.

Complacent in its wealth, disdainful of its poor, violent with one another, Scripture says they "added house to house and field to field" by totally dishonest means, and with sinful disregard for the effects of it all on the widows, orphans, and dispossessed.

The leadership called it "progress." The priests called it "blessing." The wealthy called it "good times." But Isaiah called it "sin" and withdrew to teach a small band of the faithful to think as he did so that when Yahweh's plan to purge that sick society had been fulfilled a small candle of truth, of hope, would still burn in a burned out world. He could not win the day but he did not give up the struggle. He did not give in to ideas that destroyed. He did not accept situations that compromised him. He did not buy into the marshmallow mentality that passed for patriotism and piety in those around him. He kept on keeping on, fanning small flames, lighting small fires, being the small voice of another truth in a world on the rampage. Through it all, Isaiah held on, went on, carried on, seeing little success, exerting great effort, giving his entire life to an apparently fruitless task that was right only because it was right. And he went on even when things seemed most bleak and life seemed most futile and the values he cherished seemed most lost.

The Courage to Speak Out

God knows, we need the endurance of an Isaiah now.

Isaiah would be at home in Detroit. He would recognize Washington, D.C. He could find his way around Chicago very well. Isaiah would fathom the meaning of the small abandoned farms and the closed-down factories in these places in ways that most of us do not. He would smell from miles away the cash-crop money and the contrived Third World debt payments and the ill-gotten oil from war profits that are pouring into the financial centers of Wall Street to maintain the powerful. And he would be sickened by it all. And he would say so. Over and over again.

We, too, need the holy imagination and the indomitable spirit of Isaiah to create a new mentality in a society that has come to take for granted wealth for those who can get it and destitution for those who can not.

We are not the first people to excuse ourselves from responsibility for our own reality, of course. We are not the first people to ignore the situation around us, sure that we, of all neighbors, will feel no results of the violence, economic and social that now engulfs us on this globe.

This is the generation whose violence will erupt in our own backyards while we sit around and wonder why unless the Isaiah in us speaks out once more.

Called to Conversion

The prophets did not wonder why Israel was floundering, despite their chosenness, despite the covenant, despite the Exodus. The prophets knew why. Israel had forgotten "the widow and the orphan," the poor and the helpless, the Word of God and the law of God. For those things they had substituted shrines and temples, sacrifices and symbols, religion for show rather than religion for real. The function of the prophets was to force the Hebrew people to face the questions, questions that we ourselves must face.

Amos and Hosea and Isaiah were all simply people of their times. Like them, we will not be given the right to absent ourselves from the call, no matter the time it takes us. "Every day I cast my seeds to the wind," an ancient story tells. "It takes no virtue to cast those seeds, of course," the farmer admits, "but it does take courage to go on facing the wind."

What is needed now in a time when the established powers are trying desperately to maintain their established positions in a rapidly changing world is the godly courage to go on casting seeds to the wind.

Discussion

1. Is it enough to endure for "endurance sake"? What are the dangers of this kind of endurance? Does anything change for you if you think of endurance as "passionate patience" or "a burning patience" or "a revolutionary patience"?

2. Name one thing you have endured in doing or in proclaiming. Are you hopeful? Hopeless? Why are you still enduring?

3. How would you define "holy imagination"? Have you ever seen it? Explain.

ECHOES: WOMEN PROPHETS

Several times I have decided to leave—I almost could except for the children, the poor bruised victims of adult lunacy. Who would care for them? Whose heart would be so staunch as to favor the reasonable thing in a sea of tears and loneliness? Not mine, dear friend, not mine.

Jean Donovan, lay Maryknoll missionary
murdered with three other women religious by the military
for defending the poor in El Salvador

Nothing could be worse than the fear that one had given up too soon and left one unexpended effort that might have saved the world.

Jane Addams, Nobel Peace Prize recipient,
suffragette and founder of Hull House

Nothing great was ever done without much enduring.

St. Catherine of Sienna

Cautious, careful people, always casting about to preserve
their reputation and social standing, never can bring about
a reform. Those who are really in earnest must be willing
to be anything or nothing in the world's estimation, and
publicly and privately, in season and out, avow their sympa-
thy with despised and persecuted ideas and their advocates,
and bear the consequences.

Susan B. Anthony

Response

Which of the voices of women prophets spoke to you most clearly? Explain.

PHOTO and POEM MEDITATION

Sit with this photo a few minutes and read the poem.

Song of the Builders

by Mary Oliver

On a summer morning
I sat down
on a hillside
to think about God—

a worthy pastime.
Near me, I saw
a single cricket;
it was moving the grains
of the hillside

this way and that way.
How great was its energy,
how humble its effort.
Let us hope

it will always be like this,
each of us going on
in our inexplicable ways
building the universe.

Creative Response

Individual:

Memorize this prayer:

> Let nothing disturb thee
> Let nothing frighten thee
> All things are changing
> God alone is changeless
> Patience attains the goal
> One who has God lacks nothing
> God alone fills all our needs.
> —Saint Teresa of Avila

Group:

1. At the meeting have each person write a note to someone they admire because of his or her endurance. Or write a short letter to the editor about this person. Thank them for having "the godly courage to go on casting seeds to the wind." Mail them. (Have note cards or postcards or stationery and envelopes available.)

2. Break into groups of three or four and do a dramatization about prophetic endurance that incorporates this story: "Every day I cast my seeds to the wind," an ancient story tells. "It takes no virtue to cast those seeds, but it does take courage to go on facing the wind." Or dramatize the Prayer of St. Teresa of Avila in relation to prophetic endurance.

Micah
The Contemplative in Action

Scripture

Listen here, mortal:
God has already made abundantly clear what "good" is,
    and what YHWH needs from you: simply do justice,
    love kindness, and humbly walk with YHWH.

Micah 6:8

But at the end of days, the mountain of YHWY's Temple
    will be established as the most important mountain
    and raised above all other hills—all nations will stream toward it.
Many people will come and say:
    "Come, let us climb YHWH's mountain
    to the Temple of the God of Jacob,
that we may be instructed in God's ways and walk in God's paths."
Instruction will be given from Zion
    and the word of YHWH from Jerusalem.
YHWH will judge between many peoples
    and arbitrate between mighty and distant nations;
They will beat their swords into plowshares,
    and their spears into pruning hooks;
one nation will not raise the sword against another,
    and never again will they train for war.
People will sit under their own vines and fig trees
    with no one to make them afraid.
    The mouth of YHWH Omnipotent has spoken.

Micah 4: 1-5

Response

Find a work of art or a picture or story in this week's media—newspaper, internet TV—that speaks about this week's scripture. Explain.

The Prophet Micah

by Joan Chittister

The development of the prophetic life in the West depends on the cultural gift of the Far East—a commitment to awareness, to presence, to what is going on before the eyes of the seeker at the present moment. Where Westerners calculate the nature of life in large, sweeping concepts, in grand theological "truths" the spiritual masters of the Far East plumb the depths of the present. The Eastern mind wrings cosmic truth out of the simplest of acts. The Zen master, in fact, has taught through the ages, "O wonder of wonders. I chop wood. I draw water from the well." What is going on now, here, at this very moment, in other words, is the stuff of spirituality. Not ideas only, not religious disciplines only, not "belief" in the academic sense of the word, not even "good acts" satisfy for the Eastern notion of "the spiritual life."

The capacity for consciousness may be exactly what is lacking in the Western soul. That may be why charity, but not prophecy, marks the religious imagination of the modern world. That may be exactly the reason why the pollution of the globe and the rise of nuclear weaponry has sprung up willy-nilly, like mushrooms after rain, in Western society: We look but we do not see. We act but we do not think. We plan but we do not reflect. We pray but we do not contemplate. We are more pragmatic than we are ethical. If it works we do it. We ask only rarely, if at all, whether what is technically possible is also morally appropriate, really life-enhancing, good for children and other living things. The whole effect is, far too often, "progress" without respect for established priorities, profit without human progress at all.

The real problem may be that we are not a contemplative people. But if that is the case, its corollary is all too clear: the real problem is that without a contemplative mode of life we will never be a prophetic people.

We talk about contemplation as if it were some kind of spiritual magic. Actually, the contemplative is the person who is so immersed in the will of God that they come to see the world as God sees the world. The fact is that all of us are called to be contemplatives.

Centeredness, awareness, contemplative presence catapult even the most average of persons from a kind of robotized existence to the very heights of humanity, to the absolute depths of the human soul. But it is precisely there, in the depths of the seeing soul, that the word of God begins to make spiritual demands.

Normalcy, compassion and endurance mark the prophetic endeavor, yes. But centeredness compels it. We need to be able to ask "why" and "with what long-term effects" and "at what cost to the values we hold most dear?" Those are the questions that preoccupy the serious Christian, that drive the saints, that impelled Micah the prophet.

The Message of Micah

The prophet Micah, the elder, was a contemplative par excellence. Micah came from the territory designed as a first line of defense for Jerusalem. He watched people being commandeered into forced labor camps to build the public works projects that served the rich. He saw clearly what was going on, and he said so: "They are skinning people alive," he shouted at the wealthy and complacent of Israel. "They are pulling the flesh off their bones, eating my people's flesh, stripping off their skin, breaking up their bones, chopping them up small—like flesh for the pot, like meat in the stew-pan."

And Micah blamed the sages and the elders for it because they did not stand up on behalf of the poor of their world. They prophesied for profit but not for truth, he said. They talked religion and philosophy but they did not live it. In fact, they used religion to buoy up a system long condemned by both their ideas and their laws. By the very distance that they had placed between themselves and the issues of the world around them, they led the people astray.

Centered in the World

And here and now what has changed? The elders of this society, our experts and consultants, our economists and elected representatives, talk in terms of charts and make predictions and give percentages and develop platforms that show without fail more success for the successful, more wealth for the wealthy. But they put no faces on the bottom lines of their graphs, no wisdom in their messages.

Instead, they preach the evil of welfare for the poor and practice the evil of welfare for the rich. They talk free enterprise and save major corporations and investment firms and banks because, they say, "They can't do it themselves." Then they talk free enterprise some more and cut funds for families with dependent children and subsidized housing and loans for education and grants for the arts because they say, "In a free enterprise society, 'Those people should do it themselves.'"

The point is not that one should be chosen over the other. The point is that though both are needs, the distribution of the goods of the earth seems mightily to depend more on who needs what than on the fact that everybody needs something.

The question for us is: Are we centered in the Word, thinking for ourselves and prophesying for the poor or are we simply following the loudest voice, the last voice, the most powerful voice?

Are we even aware that what is going on around us is part and parcel of the spiritual life that we proclaim in our liturgy but ignore in real life? Are we centered on the impact of the moment and conscious of its implications or are we simply caught up in the politics of the time whatever its values, whatever its internal contradictions?

Justice for the Oppressed

Indeed we, too, need to learn to contemplate the present in the light of the Gospel. We need to become aware of what is before us. We must begin to understand, like Micah, that the Word of God was justice, not therapy; given for meaning, not for magic; meant to change the world, not simply to make us feel good. We must learn to ask why the poor are poor, what God wants for the world, how to live well and not just successfully. We must learn to look into the eyes of the Jesus who fed the hungry, and touched lepers, and raised women, and contended with the establishment to ask what we see in those situations there that demand a prophetic word now and here. We must begin to look beneath the status quo to find the reasons for the status quo, the effects of the status quo, the sin of the status quo, the oppression that the status quo visits on the poorest of the poor.

40

The Sufi tell a tale that takes us to the heart of contemplation. Once upon a time, the disciples said to the Holy One: "Tell us what you got from enlightenment. Did you become divine?"

"No, not divine," the Holy One said.

"Did you become a saint?"

"Oh, dear, no," the Holy One said.

"Then what did you become?" the disciples asked.

"I became awake," the Holy One said.

It is one thing to be pious; it is another thing to be awake. Piety makes us feel good; justice makes the rest of the world feel good, as well.

The prophets did not come preaching piety. The prophets came demanding justice for those least able to secure it for themselves.

Awareness, clearly, becomes the springboard of the good life. Without awareness we accept as the good gold of the faith what we later come to see is only baseless dross. The prophet Micah, a contemplative to the core, calls us to contemplative action, the only authentic religious action that there is, in fact, all other religious behavior notwithstanding.

Discussion

1. How would you define a contemplative? Do you consider yourself a contemplative? Why or why not? How do you become a contemplative? Grace? Silence? Presence with the poor? Reflection on Scripture? Discipline? Prayer? Immersion in beauty? All of the above? Explain.

2. In the novel, *The Chosen*, by Chaim Potok, one of the main characters is the son of a great Hassidic Rabbi. The Rabbi doesn't speak to his son for years in order to teach the boy to go into the depth of silence until he hears the cries, the laments of the suffering world. Has this been your experience with silence?

3. List all the sources of noise in your life—news, e-mail, radio, I-pods, meetings, etc. Do these hinder or enhance your contemplative vision?

ECHOES: WOMEN PROPHETS

The fullness of joy is to behold God in everything.

Julian of Norwich

Place your mind before the mirror of eternity!
Place your soul in the brilliance of glory!
Place your heart in the figure of divine substance!
And transform your whole being into the image
of the Godhead Itself through contemplation!

St. Claire of Assisi

I never pray for anything temporal...but when each morning
comes, I kneel down before the Rising Sun, and only say,
"Behold the handmaid of the Lord–give me this day my
work to do–no, not my work, but thine."

Florence Nightingale

"...quite suddenly I saw with my mind, but as vividly as a wonderful picture, Christ in them all. But I saw more than that; not only was Christ in every one of them, living in them, dying in them, rejoicing in them, sorrowing in them– but because He was in them, and because they were here, the whole world was here too, here in the underground train.... I came out into the street and walked for a long time in the crowds. It was the same here, on every side, in every passerby, everywhere–Christ."

Vision of mystic and author Caryll Houselander
while standing in a crowded train during rush hour

Whatever I had read as a child about the saints had thrilled me. I could see the nobility of giving one's life for the sick, the maimed, the leper.... But there was another question in my mind. Why was so much done in remedying the evil instead of avoiding it in the first place?...Where were the saints to try to change the social order, not just to minister to the slaves, but to do away with slavery.

Dorothy Day

Response

Which of the voices of women prophets spoke to you most clearly? Explain.

PHOTO and POEM MEDITATION

Sit with this photo a few minutes and read the poem.

God Would Kneel Down

I think God might be a little prejudiced.
For once He asked me to join Him on a walk
through this world,

and we gazed into every heart on this earth,
and I noticed He lingered a bit longer
before any face that was
weeping,

and before any eyes that were
laughing.

And sometimes when we passed
a soul in worship

God too would kneel
down.

I have come to learn: God
adores His
creation.

St. Francis of Assisi

Creative Response

Individual:
Take a "contemplative walk" by yourself this week through some tranquil section of nature–by a lake, a mountain, a forest, etc. Then take a walk through or by a suffering section of your town or city–inner-city neighborhoods, a nursing home, a hospital, a soup kitchen. Select an object or take a photo of something that captures the essence of each walk. Contemplate both of these.

Group:
1. Bring the object or photo from your "contemplative walk" to the group. Share your "contemplative walk" experience. Then place the objects in the middle of the group and sit in silence for ten minutes reciting this mantra silently: "I have come to learn: God adores His creation."

2. Break into groups of three or four and dramatize the poem by St. Francis of Assisi.

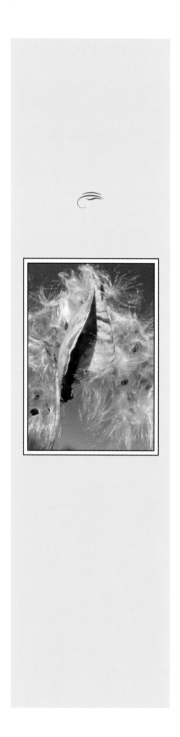

WEEK FIVE

Ezekiel
Seer of the Unseen

Scripture

Thus says SovereignYHWY: "Approach from the four winds, Breath, and breathe on these slain, that they may live."
Ezekiel 37: 9

This is what Sovereign YHWH says: I will gather you from among the nations and bring you back from the countries where you were scattered, and I will return to you the land of Israel again. When you return you will get rid of the vile idols and abominable practices. And I will give you single-ness of heart and put a new spirit in you. I will remove the heart of stone from your bodies and give you a heart of flesh. Then you will follow my decrees and carefully keep my laws. You will be my people, and I will be your God.
Ezekiel 11: 17-21

Response

Find a work of art or a picture or story in this week's media—newspaper, internet TV—that speaks about this week's scripture. Explain.

READING

The Prophet Ezekiel

by Joan Chittister

It is so easy to make God to our own image and likeness. It is so easy to see only the images we make of the Unimaginable, to the exclusion of all others. It is so easy to make God small and call that faith.

The evidence in every sector of human life makes the point all too well: open-mindedness, breadth of vision, the universal mind rise all too rarely in the human heart.

Fundamentalism, biblical literalism, reactionism and ideological extremism—all dispositions designed to freeze spiritual and social development to a given period—ride high now. The condition is not uncommon during periods of great social change and deep social stress. The situation begs for it, in fact. Given the loss of past absolutes and the shift in the social consensus on national values that come with technological development, major cultural transformations and new social realities, people cling to old certainties like shipwreck survivors to lifeboats.

It is precisely in times like those, a world in flux needs a prophetic commitment to principle in the face of practices long since gone awry or begging to be reviewed again. What the world needs then is openness to the Holy Spirit and a commitment to basic tenets of truth and justice and goodness and to the Will of God for all humankind. We need a faith that can function in the present, not a religion that mirrors the past.

It is not an easy task, this openness to the Spirit. It demands that we let go of our own ideas to make way for new manifestations of the presence of God in time. It is not a comfortable call, this invitation of God to a dark walk toward a distant future, but it is the ultimate manifestation of response to the Spirit.

The Prophet Is a Contemplative

At the time of Ezekiel, Israel had long been in a period of social tension and moral challenge. More than a decade before Ezekiel, Jeremiah had prophesied in the face of the national religion that the national religion itself was wrong, its pieties insincere, its notion of essential goodness and the guaranteed presence of God patently absurd. The country was theologically divided. God had chosen Zion as a divine dwelling place, so the Jerusalemites taught, and therefore God would never abandon it. Deuteronimists like Jeremiah, on the other hand, insisted that the presence of Yahweh depended upon the character of the soul of the people more than on the simple designation of the shrines.

The question, of course, was whether divine "election"–being chosen by God–guaranteed the nation's salvation. The question, of course, was whether or not Judaism was the only way to God. The question, of course, was whether or not faith sufficed for righteousness. What really counted in the saving scales of eternal judgment: behavior or belief? The nation had long been polarized on the issue. Some said that God was present in the world at large; others that the Jews were God's people and that God dwelt with Israel exclusively; that God was, in essence, a Jewish commodity.

The prophet Ezekiel, who was himself a Jerusalemite, made the mistake of seeing "Yahweh's glory" shining brightly over Babylon, a foreign state with a foreign culture, an enemy culture, a culture of multiple gods and threatening ideas. With that vision it became clear to Ezekiel that Yahweh was not a commodity to be captured by a single people, a particular culture. Yahweh was a presence to be revered in everyone, everywhere. This was a revolutionary way of thinking, both about Israel and about God. It was an insight that struck at the very heart of Israel's ancient certainties and reshaped the very center of Israel's identity. The message shook Israel in general and Ezekiel, in particular, to the core. The message was a hard one. It cost Ezekiel his old way of thinking, his old way of being religious, his old way of seeing God. It was, and is for all of us as well, the beginning of a new world view and a new world order that are coming not only with power but also with speed.

With that vision went the criteria for Crusades and the virtue of Holy Wars. With that insight, too, went the idea that God is a white Westerner and that the West is uniquely God's. With that argument, too, went the justification for converting Indians at the end of a sword and segregating black and brown and red and yellow people and "killing a Commie for Christ."

With that vision of God's presence and blessing on everybody, everywhere went the authorization of enemy-making as a virtue. Even for the sake of God. Even in the name of God.

The Real Enemy

In our time, then, the world is still in dire need of an Ezekiel. Our bones are dry and we need a new spirit of human cooperation within us. We defend our differences with a vengeance. We dedicate ourselves to the eradication of the other. Claiming morality and tradition and progress, we stand behind banners of concern and compassion and Christianity, but like the tip of an iceberg, commitment is simply what shows above the murky waters of our anxiety-sickened souls. Enmity is what rages in the current below.

Enmity is our real enemy. Enmity is self-destructive. Enmity poisons the human soul.

It is enmity that turns us into what we hate. The West hated Russian secrecy and became the secrecy center of the world. We hated the division of the churches and yet taught that division was a religious virtue. We hate the thought of the devaluation of life, yet we are more than willing to threaten it and deprive it and take it. We hate the thought of control and then set out to authoritarily impose our most unauthoritarian ideas. And as a result, we are divided everywhere.

An enmity mentality accepts only what we ourselves recognize as truth and declares war on anyone who doesn't share it—at the expense of the other and of our own basic principles of freedom and peace and love. As Augustine said: "The weapon with which we would attempt to destroy the enemy must first pass through our own hearts."

Our Prophetic Call

It takes the vision of Ezekiel to see good will where we do not see a similarity of ideas. It takes the courage of an Ezekiel to admit the weaknesses within us that corrupt our strength and erode our hearts. It takes openness of heart to see God everywhere and in everyone when we assume that godliness is common only to us, to our groups and our nation and our church and our ideas.

Vision and courage and openness to the Spirit call us to breadth of vision, to softness of heart, to the expansion of our souls beyond our parochial worlds and chauvinistic politics and segregated social lives and intellectual blandness that mask as faith and parade as religion. Ezekiel dared to think a new thought: God does not want destruction of the people of God in the name of God. And that insight into the God of love brought him pressure, rejection and personal pain. But the rest of us began to see God differently and that idea is still changing the world, changing the church.

Discussion

1. Name one new thought or new possibility or new insight or new vision that has entered your consciousness in the last year. How did you get it? Did you act on it? If you can't think of one, does that bother you? Why or why not?

2. Write the words "I imagine a world..." 15 times down a sheet of paper. Then finish the sentences. Don't think too much. Just write what comes into your head. Now circle one idea that appeals to you. What one action can you take to make your vision come true?

3. Name five people you can talk to about new ideas or controversial subjects. Call one of them up and meet them for coffee or tea or lunch. Make it a point to discuss an issue that is important to you. Do this once a month.

ECHOES: WOMEN PROPHETS

My soul proclaims your greatness, O God,
and my spirit rejoices in you, my Savior.
For you have looked with favor upon your lowly servant....
You have shown strength with your arm,
you have scattered the proud in their conceit,
you have deposed the mighty from their thrones,
and raised the lowly to high places.
You have filled the hungry with good things,
while you have sent the rich away empty.

Mary of Nazareth

Christianity is being concerned about your fellow man, not building a million-dollar church while people are starving right around the corner. Christ was a revolutionary person, out there where it was happening. That's what God is all about, and that's where I get my strength.

Fannie Lou Hammer

I know that a new and kinder day will come. I would so much like to live on, if only to express all the love I carry within me. And there is only one way of preparing the new age, by living it even now in our hearts.

Etty Hillesum

The job of the peacemaker is to stop war, to purify the world, to get it saved from poverty and riches, to heal the sick, to comfort the sad, to wake up those who have not yet found God, to create joy and beauty wherever you go, to find God in everything and in everyone.

Muriel Lester

Response

Which of the voices of women prophets spoke to you most clearly? Explain.

PHOTO and POEM MEDITATION

Sit with this photo a few minutes and read the poem.

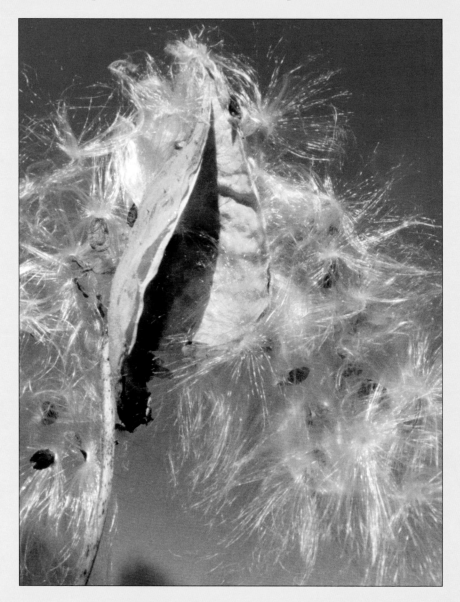

Beginners

But we have only begun
to love the earth.

We have only begun
to imagine the fullness of
life.

How could we tire of hope?
—so much is in the bud.

How can desire fail?
—we have only begun

to imagine justice and mercy,
only begun to envision

how it might be
to live as siblings

with beast and flower,
not as oppressors.

Surely our river
cannot already be hastening
into the sea of nonbeing?

Surely it cannot
drag, in the silt,

all that is innocent?
Not yet, not yet—
there is too much broken
that must be mended,
too much hurt we have done
to each other
that cannot yet be forgiven.

We have only begun to know
the power that is in us
if we would join
our solitudes in the
communion of struggle.

So much is unfolding that must
complete its gesture,

Denise Levertov

Beginners
Dedicated to the memory of Karen Silkwood
and Eliot Gralla

"From too much love of living,
Hope and desire set free,
Even the weariest river
Winds somewhere to the sea—"

Creative Response

Individual:
Find a hymn or popular song that visions a new heaven and a new earth. For example, "Imagine" by John Lennon, "Blowin in the Wind" by Bob Dylan, "What a Wonderful World" by Louie Armstrong, any Easter hymn. Listen to it. If you feel called, do some body movement to the song.

Group:
1. Have different pairs of glasses available (find them in dollar stores). Have each participant put on a pair of glasses. Assign each person a role: Politician, scientist, artist, religious leader, writer, teacher, CEO of major corporation, mother of five, factory worker, illegal immigrant, homeless person, elderly person, person on parole, etc. On a sheet of paper, have each person list five ways—from their perspective—to make the earth a more just and peaceful place. Have each person share their list.

Task: as a group you must come up with A NEW VISION FOR TOMORROW and agree on 5 goals for this new world. Once you have decided, read your goals aloud. Then have each person say aloud one action they will do to make the vision a reality.

2. Break into groups of three or four and dramatize one or all of this week's "Echoes: Voices of Women Prophets." Or do a choral reading of this week's poem by Denise Levertov.

Jesus
The Prophetic Reign of God

Scripture

When the Sabbath was over, Mary of Magdala, Mary the mother of James, and Salome brought perfumed oils so that they could anount Jesus. Very early, just after sunrise on the first day of the week, they came to the tomb.

They were saying to one another, "Who will roll back the stone for us from the entrance to the tomb?" When they looked, they found that the huge stone had been rolled back.

On entering the tomb, they saw a young person sitting on the right, dressed in a white robe. They were very frightened, but the youth reassured them: "Do not be amazed! You are looking for Jesus of Nazareth, the One who was crucified. He has risen; he is not here. See the place where they laid him. Now go and tell the disciples and Peter, 'Jesus is going ahead of you to Galilee, where you will see him just as he told you.'"

Mark 16: 1-8

Jesus the Prophet

by Joan Chittister

The line of prophets is a long and impressive one: Amos, Hosea, Isaiah, Micah, Ezekiel all speak of things we know only too well yet. We live in a world teeming with wealth and weighed down by the sight of the poor. We understand militarism in all its masquerading forms: patriotism, national security, liberation, and the so-called preemptive response set off by fear. We know what prejudice and parochialism and provincialism can do in a society where people come in many colors, talk in many languages, see the world through many filters, experience life in many ways–as female as well as male, old as well as young, poor as well as rich, non-Christian as well as Christian.

The voices of the prophets ring down the centuries yet to warn us of these things, to enlist us in the chorus of no's it will take to change the world in which we live so that the world God intended for us all may finally come to fullness for us all.

They call us to be alert to our responsibilities to the poor while we're intent on making profit for ourselves. They remind us of the need for compassion, however much we make conviction the hallmark of our lives. They remind us that constancy is more a part of prophecy than flamboyant but momentary courage. They call us to constant reflection so that in our zeal for the will of God we do not fall into the temptation to substitute our own word for the Word of God. They require us to follow the vision of God beyond even our own boundaries, our own kind.

They challenge us to this day, of course. But even with all of their intensity, it is Easter Sunday that brings us the greatest prophetic message of them all. On Easter Sunday, prophecy rises from the grave, eternal and triumphant, unfinished but unrelenting. The sight of the empty tomb prods us to go on prophetically ourselves creating creation anew according to the mind of God.

A Witness to Life

When Jesus rises from the tomb, he says to Mary Magdalen in the garden, "Go and tell Peter and the others that I have gone before you into Galilee and I will meet them there." The words are prophetic ones for us all. Jesus does not promise to meet the disciples in Jerusalem, at the center of power and profit, as an Establishment figure of either state or synagogue, as the vindicated and recognized one. No, the last act of Jesus is to lead the disciples to the Galilee, to the backwaters of Israel, to the hinterlands of the poor and dispossessed, to the forgotten and the oppressed ones. Where he had spent his public life on behalf of the forgotten one, he expects us to spend ours.

When Jesus ascends from this life to Life in the heart of God, the angels say to the disciples who witness this final passage from life to Life, "Why do you stand looking up to heaven?" (Acts 1:11) The question is a haunting one, a prophetic one: Why do we stand around waiting for something to save us from ourselves? We are the ones who made nuclear weapons; we are the ones who can decide to stop making them. We are the ones who pass the legislation that advantages the rich and empoverishes the poor. We can demand better. We are the ones who can pass the bills that would give them the essentials of life—food, housing, education. We are the ones who make war, not peace, who torture in the name of God and call degradation justice, who make life cheap from womb to tomb. And we are the ones who can forbid such inhumanity, can disavow such political policies, can demand justice and equality and peace.

If only we will.

And yet, if we do not, what has Easter really been about? If we do not witness to life over death, then what is the empty tomb really all about? If we refuse to persevere until all the oppression stops and all the discrimination ends and all the inequality is over, then what was the life of the Prophet Jesus really all about for us? Today and now and here.

Easter is about the triumph of life over death, of the mind of God over the plans of a humanity gone awry, over the strategies of sin enthroned in both church and state.

Jesus the Prophet leaves us to complete the prophetic word in our own time.

Easter is not about the end of anything. It is about the beginning of the prophetic reign of God. But it cannot happen unless we ourselves leave the site of the tomb and go to the streets and the hovels and the powerful of our own time and say a prophet's word.

We are the normal people Jesus calls to speak the message again. We are the passionate ones who are called now to speak it over and over, with persistence and with confidence. To speak it courageously on behalf of those who suffer. To speak it compassionately with care, even for those who do not speak it at all. To speak it with a vision that transcends the limits of our own language and tribe, system and circumstances.

The prophetic dimension of Easter does not end with Jesus, it starts with us.

The spiritual journey that hears the cry of the prophets and sees that cry fulfilled in Jesus and heeds that cry in our own time is the journey we are meant to make. Otherwise, why go from Galilee to Golgatha, from Upper Room to the Tomb at all?

Alleluia, we sing at the tomb. Alleluia all our lives. We are alleluia people who go through life praising God and following Jesus till the Garden of Gethsemani is turned into the Garden of Eden again.

We know what the life of Jesus was about. Now it is time to ask ourselves whether our own lives begin to match it in message and meaning. We must ask ourselves, standing at an empty tomb, under an empty cross, in front of a needy world, whether or not when people see us at work in this time, they can say Alleluia, too.

Acknowledgments

To learn more about women prophets, read *Blessed Among Women* by Robert Ellsberg, Editor-in-Chief of Orbis Books.

(Published by Crossroad, it is available at www.ipgbook.com)

Many of the quotes used in the "Echo: Women Prophets" were taken from his book.

✠

An earlier version of the reflections on the prophets by Joan Chittister appeared in 1995 as a five-part series in the *Liguorian* magazine.

Poetry Credits

Page 15 "Call and Answer" by Robert Bly. Reprinted from *My Sentence Was a Thousand Years of Joy*, Harper Collins, New York, 2005. Copyright 2005 Robert Bly. Used with his permission.

Page 25 "The Way They Held Each Other" by Mira from the Penguin anthology *Love Poems from God*, copyright 2002 Daniel Ladinsky and used with his permission.

Page 35 "Song of the Builders" by Mary Oliver from *Why I Wake Early* copyright Beacon Press. Reprinted with permission.

Page 45 "God Would Kneel Down" by St. Francis of Assisi from the Penguin anthology *Love Poems from God*, copyright 2002 Daniel Ladinsky and used with his permission.

Page 55 "Beginners" by Denise Levertov from *Candles in Babylon*, New Directions, 1982. Used with permission.

Scripture Credit

All scripture translations are from *The Inclusive Hebrew Scriptures, Volume II, the Prophets* and *The Inclusive New Testament* by Priests for Equality, a project of the Quixote Center. Now available in one volume, *The Inclusive Bible*, Sheed and Ward, information at www.quixote.org Used with permission.

Photography Credits

Cover Art Becker (abecker@artbeckerphoto.com)

Page 14 Carolyn Gorny-Kopkowski, OSB

Page 24 Marian Wehler, OSB

Page 34 Bernadette Sullivan, OSB

Page 44 Stephanie Schmidt, OSB

Page 54 Ann Muczynski, OSB

Page 57 Stephanie Schmidt, OSB